SOME OF THE TIMES

Gina Myers

Published by Barrelhouse Books
Baltimore, MD

www.barrelhousemag.com

Published in the United States of America
ISBN 13: 978-0-9889945-8-4

First Edition

Cover design & collage: Shanna Compton, from photos by Jaime Torres (*New Plantation Blues*, by permission of artist) and Samuel Mann (Philadephia, 2011; licensed under CC BY 2.0)
Page design: Tony Mancus

TO DO

Tune out the 6pm/10pm news
Open your home to friends & comrades, share food & stories
Don't forget to listen to music & make art
They aren't prepared for the sound of our voices
Remove yourself from the slow drain of 9-to-5,
the dull lights of the subway, the stop & start,
bright advertisements for value meals
& dental surgeons
Reject the language they use to justify privilege
& explain away disadvantage
the language that expects us to behave, stay in line,
be placated by a paycheck
Remember that the time is yours, is ours
It belongs to us
Refuse to be defined by outside forces
Don't be afraid to fail in trying to forge a new way
Try again & again as if your life depends on it
Your life does depend on it
Remember di Prima: *you can have what you ask for, ask for / everything*

RISK TRANSFER

South Philly front
stoop social club
We share some beer
& laugh into the
night / Words
failing in our need
to express
our fears, or why
we're sitting here
waiting
on the destruction
of everything

How much is a
concept of security
worth to you?
By which I mean
fuck the police
Existence legitimized
through buying power
Public space closing
in favor of commercial
development
The city calls
its citizens taxpayers
& installs dividers
in the middle of
park benches

to keep people
from lying down
& staying too long

We sit
on the stoop
& ask who said love
can save us?
Can love save us?
The day passes
before us
Shards of glass
& splintered wood
scatter
across the street
as the garbage truck
crushes a mirror
& lets the refuse fall

EMMA

Mid-May, 90 degrees. Severe
thunderstorm watch.
Outside of the subway station,
teenagers hand out flyers
for a politician. This week
already long, only Tuesday.
Yesterday's medical tests
left me nauseated & sick
in bed. I missed
the poetry reading.
I missed the concert, I missed
yoga. A hidden cost
of illness: the things I spend
money on but don't go to.
Emma sends me an article
about the discovery of rocks
formed from plastic.
I send Emma an article
about trees having a heartbeat.
No one I know knows
how to function right now.
Every day at least one
new horror in the news.
Emma asks, "What keeps you
going?" Yesterday
Palestinian protesters
were slaughtered in Gaza.
Today: business as usual.

I have a meeting. I meet Erin
for lunch. I read my emails.
I work on the report.
I tell Emma: poetry,
music & friends. The sky,
a minute ago, sunny. Suddenly
dark as the storm comes.
The truth is, Emma, I don't know
what keeps me going
right now. The wind picks up,
howls down the alley
behind my apartment.
I hear my neighbor's footsteps
above me. I wonder if he heard me
cry last night when I was
feeling alone with my illness.
My friends tell me I'm not
alone, but I still feel this way.
I was surprised
by the sudden tears
at the bar on Sunday. We
were talking about rents in Philly
& I didn't even know
I had begun to cry until my voice
cracked. The radio
loses its signal to the storm.
When friends say they're sorry
for what I'm going through,
I always say, "It's okay. It will be fine."
I say things I don't believe
but believe I'm supposed to say.

The teenagers now running
down the street, seeking shelter.
Thunder & the downpour begins.
I was taught to never ask
for help. My dad mistaking this
for strength. It's okay.
It will be fine. The radio
has found its signal again. Dear Emma,
it's okay. It will be fine.
The radio: static. Now: silence.

NEW YEAR'S DAY (2018)

champagne bottle   shattered
    on 4th Ave.   paper silver
crown
        flattened
9 degrees & it's good   to see you
        we warm up
over ramen   2 cups
of tea & memories   of faraway beaches
    riding the train   into Manhattan
I seek a shape   to place
        my desire into
it's my heart   that leaves
    first   *do you remember*
what it was like
        to live here?   capital
gleams   off the buildings
Philadelphia far   away
    what is   the opposite of
a resolution
        a dissolution
            a disillusion

PHILADELPHIA

New city same shit
Moving through
the streets
pre-fall golden
in late afternoon
sunlight / bright red
crumbling brick
& shoddy graffiti
asks *freedom?*
Each year I fight
& each year
the things that hold
me back feel stronger
Shirking the day's
responsibilities
to sit by the river
this afternoon
I wouldn't give this
up but no it's not
freedom

We can go
to the coast
It's a short drive
We'll make believe
a getaway vacation
& walk the boardwalk
& in the morning
I'll take you
to the airport
Everything is
fleeting
& it makes life
more interesting
We will have fun
until we won't

It was a song
that claimed
the ocean
would wash away
my problems

I thought
I could find
freedom in
a book
but I was wrong
Now it's the dream
of the road
to go & never
stop / Now it's
the moment
at the end of
the work day
when I take off
my dress

Summer
heat thick
as streetlight
shines in
the kitchen window
where I dance
to old soul songs
The love I feel
is not a freedom
from pain
It allows me
to better feel
pain / I love
the pain
the pain in these
old songs
the pain I feel
at night

There is
no breeze
I do not
put myself
forward / I'm
just here
walking down
the sidewalk
refusing
to make sense
of things
that can't be
made sense of
& appreciating
my insignificance
She said it was
when she knew
she wasn't special
that she could
write poems
A lot of people
want to be
somebody
I just want
to get through
the day

At the baseball
game the drinks
keep coming
& we are losing
badly but hardly
notice / The sun
bright as it burns
The day still joyful
& full of life,
such a surprise

In America
they shoot kids
in the street
In Ferguson
journalists
are told they're
endangering
their lives
by being there
Others are
endangering
their lives
simply by being
This declared
no fly zone
guarantees
no aerial news
coverage
The militarized
police free
to do whatever
I don't know
how we go on
Maybe we don't

What do you do
when the news
makes you sick,
when living feels
impossible
everyday passing
the graffiti
that asks, *freedom?*

Clouds crowd
out the sunlight
but I'm going to sit
inside a dark bar
anyway / I don't
trust my phone
but I take it with me
everywhere
My dad thinks
if my grandma
had lived longer
I would have found
religion or at least
have fewer tattoos
Even so he says
he's proud
of the way I up
& leave when I want
even when
I have no reason
to stay or be
anywhere

Hey baby
come sit on
my lap / Why
don't you smile
Oow I could
get me some
of that
You got a
boyfriend
Bitch, you know
you want it
Dumb cunt

If I live longer
I can pay down
some more debt
If I live longer
I can accrue
some more debt
It's okay to not
know how to be
happy / I watch
automatic sprinklers
run in the rain
while the residents
of Detroit go
without water
Once at the bar
a guy showed me
a video of a woman
pushing gummy
worms out of her
vagina / I think
he was coming
onto me / We had
very different views
He said, *Obama
can take my guns
from my cold
dead hands*
I went dead space
& thought about
gummy worms

My new boss
likes my tattoos
This week
I walked
into a bar &
everyone there
knew my name
I don't have to kiss
every guy I spend
an evening
talking with
but I can
if I want to
& they consent
I know it's dumb
to say but
the Tigers are
breaking
my heart
It happens each fall
My boss asked me
what tattoo I'll get
when I leave
Philadelphia
I've lived here
one month but
she already knows
I'll leave / If I don't
keep moving
I'll die

I don't want
to hear it
if I can't
dance to it
Stevie sings
you can feel
it all over
& it's joyful
& the joy takes
me & I feel it
all over

Fall comes
& reassures me
with its Sunday
rituals / He said
freedom would be
being able to swim
in any body
of water
clean, free of
pollution—
to be able to
reach your hands
in the river
& take a drink
I said, tonight
I'm going to listen
to every sad song
ever / This will
take me the rest
of my life
Sam sings,
bring it on home
to me

Based on
the internet
it's pretty clear
we're all fucked
& yet we go on
& continue to fall
in love / I continue
It's only when
watching football
that I find myself
yelling things like
Rip his head off
On YouTube
you can watch
videos of journalists
being beheaded
Take poetry
out of the classrooms
& into the streets
The waitress
has Liberty tattooed
on her arm
& I want to ask her
what it means

How much of
an asshole am I
that I live
somewhere
for a month
& think I can
tell its story
Every day there
is news of
a new police
brutality
What use
is love
right now?
The people
are strong
& gather
in the street
each night
I guess I'm
not telling *its*
story / I'm
just telling
a story

I was asked
to write a love
poem but instead
wrote about
loneliness
This morning
I read that love
is the fiercest
reason
for living
& I just don't
know—
it's somewhere
out of reach

The first
cold day
of the season
is here
& I wonder
how cold
my apartment
will get
this winter
This morning
I drink coffee
stand in
the rectangle
of sunlight
in the window
& look down
at the litter
collecting
at the curb
& I feel in love
with the world
I don't want
to be vulnerable
but here I am
now vulnerable

What is it
that I am
waiting for?
Not a thing
that I know
Maybe to feel
at home here
or anywhere
Today I priced
flights to Michigan
but they were
too expensive
Skimmed job ads
She said people
don't want to
get too close
because
I always leave
Or maybe I'm
never fully here
It's the little
thin things
& I try to see
them but
sometimes
I can't

JUMP SHOT

My phone was stolen
& I came to realize
how many times
in the day I stop
to take a picture.
Good news though:
no more unsolicited
dick pics. Strolling
through South Philly
tripped up over
uneven sidewalks, rolled
ankles. The sound of
a car alarm down the street.
At the park the hoops
have no nets but no one
cares. The jump shot
so smooth & carefree
as if the court counters
everything in life off
the court. We laugh
& high five & then it's back
to our separate lives
bills to pay, groceries,
the things that keep me
restless at night.
Saturday is like heaven,
endless free hall pass.
It's easy to want to

stay in bed but I'm all
Fuck that. Let's do something.
The day is ours & how
often is that the case.
We ride the lights
into the night, singing
along to our favorite songs
& I wish the night
would never end,
no, let's not let it end.

5.16.14

Whenever someone says
for better or worse, they always
mean worse. You like the song
because you know someone good
who died young, but what
does that say about us still here?
Once basketball season ends,
I'm not sure what's left to live for.
I'm tired of the war on women & the war
on the poor & on minorities & labor
& drugs. My business casual attire
isn't very punk rock, I know.
I meant to say Wilfred Owen
but instead said Owen Wilson.
What is this culture? The computer
makes me stupider each day.
I have to remind myself that I don't need
to control the way people talk
about my city. I'll see your American
exceptionalism & raise my American
denialism. I just wanted you to know
you looked so fucking punk lighting
a cigarette in your author photo.

8.8.16

again   we complain
         about the heat
summer   brain dead
            floating
in the pool   head empty
like a pop song
            if every day
              were this simple
              the mountains
              on my beer can
           turn blue
        when it's cold
american ingenuity
                the cockroaches
seek refuge on the sidewalk
at night
                at the bar
some guy says
        writing is no big deal
everyone can write
& I look at my phone
& send my boyfriend
a video of a dog
with prosthetic legs

RENT SONNET

I wrote the rent check from the wrong account
& almost got evicted when it bounced.
Now each month I bring my rent in 20s
from the ATM to the corner store my landlord
owns where he overcharges for everything—
$5 for a 10 oz. brick of Bustelo?
I miss the glory days of youth where I didn't
pay for groceries & ate whatever was put before me.
My phone vibrates with the latest sports news—
trade talks & suspensions. Somebody's
quarterback was arrested. American violence
proliferated across every media. Reposted
across platforms. Frowny emoji face.
Angry face. A president who exclaims, "Sad!"
This year let's skip all the reunions & be
with the ones we love & make love all night long.

FOURTH OF JULY (2013)

Listening to The Clash
"I'm So Bored with the USA"
on repeat. I'm too old to believe
in five minute abs. I thought
the neon sign said OPEN
but when I got closer I saw
it said GYRO & was closed.
Rainy holiday in Atlanta, sleepy
gray day while what looks
like a revolution takes place
in Egypt. Each year it gets harder
for me to believe in anything.
Tonight it is getting harder
for me to believe anything.
And tonight there will be
murders in my hometown,
the boom of fireworks
covering the pop of guns.
The land gun-crazed, drunk,
covered in empty shells.
Home of the brave.

IN CUBA

Money is always
on my mind, but I'd rather
do without it. In Cuba,
life felt easier, happier,
but don't say that
in front of the bartender.
Her dad spent 2 years
in forced labor camps
before escaping to the U.S.
I lost my iPhone in the Plaza
de la Revolución. Later I read
about the CIA sabotaging
Cuba's sugarcane & killing
their pigs. In English, Estéban
acknowledges, "Yes, a dark
history." Sometimes words
in any language come up short.
Now in Santa Cruz, I sit
along the Pacific Ocean
& imagine a new way to live.
Next week in Philly, I'll be
back to work & my old way
of living. Let's abolish debt!
And rent! And money!
Let humans come first.
We can do it, honey!

A NOTE FROM THE WET BANDITS

I've been sick
for two weeks
but America
has been sick
its whole life.
America will
always choose
a rich white kid
over two guys
living in their van.
We were victims
of Reagan's trickle-
down economics,
victims of layoffs,
the move to overseas
manufacturing,
& home foreclosures.
Victims of a society
where profit is
more important
than people &
there's no respect
for the working,
no dignity in work.
And victims too
of that goddamn kid
who struck me
in the face

with a hot iron.
And what happened
next? America
laughed. Laughed
in our faces.
They said we didn't
deserve to get ours.
And that's all we
wanted really—
to step up & take
a little piece of the pie.
And how would it
have mattered?
That family could
replace everything
we would have
taken. Their
insurance policy
a comfort to keep
them warm, tucked
into their fancy beds
while we try
to sleep in a van
without heat.
And so I'm asking
here, America,
who is the criminal?
Who is the laughing
stock? And how
do you sleep at night?

SNOW DAY

Easily distracted
by the diamonds
          in the floor tiles.
          This winter day
everything
has come to a standstill
in Atlanta. The ice weighs down
the tree branches outside
the window, and further out:
          the empty streets.
          A lone Chevy truck fishtails
as it approaches a stop sign.
Days like this everything
feels slowed down
          & I can forget
for a while the rent check due.
I can forget that there is anything happening
outside of the walls of my brain.
Just Sunday
we sat at Lillian's, drinking
leftover champagne.
The sun a respite
from what
already felt like a long winter.
And it was easy to pretend
it was summer, the popping
bottles fireworks on the 4th
of July—the grill fired up.
But now the mood

has turned elsewhere,
as January's high hopes
fizzle into February's
          day-to-day. *It's best
not to flatter the new year*, says Schuyler.
Better to call it Mutt.

3.3.17

Today at the store
I used my phone
to calculate equivalencies
how many ounces
in a cup
simple things I never
learned & I still managed
to make a mistake
came home with
16 more ounces
of chicken broth than
needed / M would have
a field day with this
making fun of my mistake
& I would feel embarrassed
dumb & unworthy of his love
And it would be true
I'd be dismissed
because he couldn't
see a future with me
I don't blame him
I can't see my own future
never have tried to live
much beyond the present
Why was I with him
anyway? He didn't even
like Nina Simone

Said she's too intense
As if intensity in a woman
is not to be admired
or perhaps a little is okay
but not too much
To be singularly focused
It's not arguing
It's just a conversation

4.8.14

When I was young
there were nine planets
but now there are fewer.
What is there to be
certain of. Only this:
the desire to feel your
body against mine
at least once more.
Each year I need less.
I don't need your theories
to understand my lived
experience. There is
an anger I carry
inside that I will never
let go of. Something basic
to hold onto while everything
else disappears.

7.22.14

I don't believe in the beauty industry
because it doesn't believe in me.
I didn't need your TED Talk on material
possessions to know the value of things
in life. When used in a hashtag,
puncture wound is one word.
On the radio, the news cuts
from a story on water shut-offs in Detroit
to a story on Emmy nominations. I don't know
how anyone can still be sane.
It's often too much to expect the ones
you love to love you back. This week my goal
is to unsubscribe from everything.

SONNET

I didn't hear you come in last night
How was the concert? Did you get your kiss?
The night, tonight, is nothing but potential
The day only beginning now
wide open & undeterred
What are we to do?
And what of all the news yesterday brought?
I want to center myself in the present
The bird chirping now, the still Northern California air
Quiet stretches well out before me
Bernadette says, for some people it's easy to jump
from thought to thought but that doesn't mean what they say
will be interesting

SAGINAW (A DOCUMENTARY)
photos by Jaime Torres, from New Plantation Blues

A sign left behind on a building long closed. Empty parking lots stretch for miles. Cracked sidewalks & broken streetlights. Pieces of glass scattered across the pavement. Each month, we take a toll of what businesses have closed & which houses have been abandoned or put up for sale in the neighborhood. Currently, on a single block: the house next door, the house across the street & the one next door to it. Further down, the house that has been for rent for five months now. Plus the two houses on the corner for sale & two more down the street.

No one ever promised us anything, but we had imagined a life for ourselves, a place to call home. Morning breaks behind the apartment building. Punching out at the end of the work day, a short drive home, meat & potatoes for dinner & the evening news. Go to bed & start over again. It doesn't seem like we're asking for much. I just want to follow in my father's and my father's father's footsteps. Now: no jobs, no idea of home. I just want to go to bed & start over again.

It had been grand. Once there had been money. To hear my dad talk about the Saginaw he grew up in is to hear of a completely different Saginaw than the one I grew up in. He tells me about the places he used to hang out, where he shot pool, where he & his sisters saw The Temptations & Johnny Cash, where the MC5 used to play. I can't picture the buildings. "Where are these places?" I ask. He drives by & points to empty lots. For years the city's solution to blight was to tear everything down. They said the property was worth more as a lot, but the lots sit unused.

The money that flowed in this city once supported an art museum, a zoo, a cultural center, a public transportation system. Now, all of these things rely on private donors. The art museum, after undergoing an expansion just a few years ago, is on the brink of bankruptcy & can't afford to stay open. The fairground's grand entrances stay locked. Are forgotten.

To be forgotten. To live in shadows. God is not here. No one is listening. Businesses close, people leave. First we close the public schools, then we tear down the churches. The city smaller & smaller each year.

Someone was there to take a picture. But what is it worth? A picture can be scanned, cropped & altered. It is removed from its context. Why did the photographer frame the shot this way? What lies just outside the frame? In photo after photo, the people are missing, but there are people here. There is an elementary school across the street. Every day children walk past, play outside at recess. You can hear their voices, laughter. The photograph captures a single moment, but it does not tell the whole story. A picture is not worth a thousand words. Sometimes, there are no words.

When does bearing witness become exploitative? When does action take place? When do we stop saying, "Look here, look here," & start saying, "We must do something about this"? In March 2009, the Saginaw Habitat for Humanity decided its efforts would be better spent dismantling homes, instead of building them. Their volunteers who are trained to put homes together learned to work in reverse, pulling out the nails, instead of hammering them in. Stripping siding, pipes & copper. Anything reusable. They committed to tearing down two houses per week, each week, for two years. That's 208 houses when all is said & done. In the meantime, they will also build or refurbish eight homes a year. *The New York Times* reported there were at least 800 empty houses in Saginaw, while local estimates were upward of 3,000.

What happens to a single-industry town when the industry leaves? Shortly after the industry leaves, the people leave too. The last census reported 56,000 residents in the city of Saginaw, half of what it once was. When the new census comes out, some expect to see the population drop below 50,000. City services stretch thinner & thinner. The bus comes once every two hours now.

Sometimes you can walk entire city blocks & never encounter another person. Potter Street, a once heavily commercial block, is a present-day ghost town. Store fronts smashed out. Garbage & debris litter the streets & sidewalks. Eerie silence, like an old film. The street could be cut off the grid & no one would notice. Weeds push through the broken pavement, push deep into the veins until the numbness takes over. A constant insistence on the present. There is no future. Remind yourself: This is not a dream.

Gray skies, gray skies, gray skies. What is a depression? Mental or economic? During times of recession, second-hand stores, pawn shops & shoe repair shops always see an increase in business. Here, even our pawn shops can't survive. A hollow, as in a depression in the ground. An emptiness. There are no grocery stores or corner stores in large sections of the city. You have to take a bus to buy an apple & there's no telling when the bus will come. What kind of toll does this take on a person? On a child? How is this trauma overcome?

Peel back the layers. White reveals blue reveals green reveals wood. The house was once a home, & once empty, it became a playground, then it became a squat, & then it became a drug den. Soon it will be engulfed in flames.

Sometimes it feels impossible to live here. Does this place even exist? Yet we go on. People fall in love, get married, have kids, & those kids grow up here as we grow older. We get by. I don't know that getting by is living, but I don't know what else there is to do. For weeks after I walked through the burned-out homes, all my dreams were of ash.

The local news is obsessed with what they call "firebugs." Arson is a hobby. Particularly hot times are the night before Halloween, known as Devil's Night, & the summer months. Each spring, the news will report, "The firebugs are out early this year." A few years ago we garnered national attention with an impressive 30 arsons in one night & a total of 45 arsons over a two-day period. Now: we try to board up the empty houses & mark them with yellow "Arson Watch" signs. On Devil's Night, packs of citizens walk the streets in hope of preventing more fires.

In Theodore Roethke's poem, "The Saginaw Song," he makes light of alcoholism, bar brawls, local criminals & aristocracy. He writes, "In Saginaw, in Saginaw / There's never a household fart, / For if it did occur, / It would blow the place apart." Violence has always been here, teeming under the surface, ready to erupt. Half the city turns its back on the other half of the city, sitting comfortably in front of the TV right now. Keep the front doors locked.

We can't escape this reminder of what once was. There was a time when we thought we had been promised something: a future. It was only later, when we stood in the shadow of giants, that we realized we had never been promised anything. And what is more: We learned we are disposable. But it is difficult to move on, difficult to find something new, when we are always haunted by the past. Carrying the weight. The heaviness of silenced machines & production lines bearing down on a soul. Stop.

SOME OF THE TIMES I ALMOST DIED (REAL & IMAGINED)

for Ryan Eckes who told me, "It's important to celebrate your birthday because you're going to die."

I regularly confuse the details of the story of when I stopped breathing and needed to have a spinal tap. I call my mom to straighten it out, but it turns out they're two separate stories: one happened at 8 weeks old, the other at 6 months.

+

At 12 years old, hanging out on B's porch, the slow roll of a car passes by. It turns the corner only to return again. B's mom makes us go inside & lay on the floor, wait a half hour to make sure the trouble is clear. Later that night, B's mom gets into a fistfight with a neighbor & gets her earring ripped out. Hours after that the cops come.

+

Another time at B's we are too cool for everything. Eight of us girls are walking down the middle of the street, a white van with no back windows rolls up on us & we take off running, cutting through yards & hopping fences because we heard that was the van that had abducted the girl from school.

+

Seventeen: My parents were gone for the week. I had wanted to die for a long time. I planned to do it on Wednesday night after I got home from my shit job. Alcohol & pills. But then, just a few days before, M shot himself & everything changed. That Wednesday night I drove for hours, lost, looking for my boyfriend at his college, everything a blur.

+

In 1997, Fiona Apple accepts an MTV Music Video Award & in her acceptance speech, she says, "It's just stupid that I am in this world." I realize now that she was talking about the music industry, but I always misremembered her as having said that some people are too beautiful to live in this world & she's one of them—she's too beautiful & too authentic to exist in this bullshit world—and I die & die & die of embarrassment & can never bring myself to listen to her music ever again.

+

Later, in Brooklyn: I walked into my neighborhood bodega to buy toilet paper after work. It wasn't until I turned around that I realized I had walked into a robbery or shakedown of some sort. Six men with baseball bats stood silent, staring straight ahead at the clerk, waiting for me to leave. Their trouble wasn't with me. I put my head down, walked to the front of the store, left $1.50 on the counter & walked out.

+

All over the news there was a story about a man in Florida who had eaten another man's face off. Bath salts were in the headlines. I was walking home late at night—not too late, close to midnight. I heard footsteps running up quick behind me & turned to see a man who flew right past me but then came to a stop. He was clearly wrecked on something & asked to use my phone. I told him I didn't have one. He said if he were black I would have given him my phone & then went on a long racist rant, which ended with him telling me that he might be an angel & I shouldn't treat angels this way. I said, "I don't think angels would be racist." We were walking on a bridge over the expressway, coming up on the Georgia Power building which has a tall fence along its property line. I didn't have anywhere to go, so I slowed down, trying to create distance between us. We continued in the same direction—he was about 5 feet in front of me, turning back & yelling at me the entire time. Then he stopped & took his shoes off & tossed them one at a time over the fence. About 20 feet later, he ripped his shirt off Hulk Hogan style & threw it over the fence. Luckily I didn't see what happened next because I finally reached a side street, quietly ducked off & made my way home.

+

At 29: It wasn't exactly alcohol poisoning, by which I mean I didn't go to the hospital, but I did drink a lot of whiskey & then threw up every 20 minutes for 17 hours. I convinced myself it must have been the flu.

+

I always lie to the doctor about how much I drink. I didn't realize how it would fuck up the anesthetic during surgery. I woke up screaming—I wasn't dying, but I wished I was.

+

Eighteen, twenty, twenty-eight, thirty-four: I smash a glass & press a shard into my wrist.

+

I had never truly known fear until after S was murdered. I didn't realize how much it had affected me until the first time someone unexpectedly banged on my door at night & I froze, dropped to the ground, & laid there for over an hour. Once in my current apartment, someone tried to get into the door off & on for several hours. It awoke me at 4 am & I rocked back & forth in bed, a switchblade on my nightstand, until after 8 am, when I finally yelled, "What do you want?" The person stopped pulling on the door but did not respond. They did not seem to move from outside of it. When I went out later that day, there was a single shoe & a watch, both belonging to my upstairs neighbor who had apparently had too much to drink.

+

Head over heels down a flight of stairs. Cracked skull.

+

The guidebook said not to walk on the beach alone at night because assaults are common, but we had been on the beach all night. At 7 am the sun was rising & I walked M back to the hostel & then returned to the beach to find my other friends, but they were nowhere to be seen. A man asked me to lay down with him. I said, "Thank you, but no." He grabbed my arm with both hands & tried to drag me with him. I leaned back with all my weight & we struggled for what felt like several minutes. I thought about kicking him in the balls & being done with it but I worried about being in a foreign country & didn't want to wind up in jail. I finally broke free & found my friends. One week later two women were murdered in the same area, allegedly for denying someone sex. Back home, my boyfriend suggests I take self-defense classes, which I do. And I delight in a video I have of me throwing him over my back.

NOTES & ACKNOWLEDGMENTS

Thank you to all of the editors and publications that supported this work.

"To Do" first appeared in *Mad House Magazine*, edited by Philip Mittereder. The line "you can have what you ask for, ask for / everything" is from Diane Di Prima's "Revolutionary Letter #19."

"Risk Transfer" and "3.3.17" first appeared in *Summer Stock*, edited by Andrew K. Peterson and Elizabeth Guthrie.

"Emma" and "New Year's Day (2018)" first appeared in *American Poetry Review*, edited by Elizabeth Scanlon.

Selections from "Philadelphia" appeared in *The Brooklyn Rail*, edited by Anselm Berrigan, and *Bedfellows*, edited by Jackee Sadicario, Alina Pleskova, and Laura Blagrave. "Philadelphia" was published as a chapbook by Barrelhouse—thanks to Dan Brady and Tony Mancus. The quote "the little thin things" is from Lorine Niedecker's "Paul." This poem was composed August - October 2014.

"Today" first appeared in *The Rumpus*, edited by Brian K. Spears. It also appeared on *The Poetry Project* website—thanks to Simone White.

"Jump Shot" first appeared under a different title in *Big Lucks*, edited by Mark Cugini.

"5.16.14" and "Fourth of July (2013)" appeared in *Bling That Sings*, edited by Paige Taggart.

"Rent Sonnet," "In Cuba," and "Sonnet" were first published in *The Equalizer 3.0*, edited by Michael Schiavo.

"A Note From the Wet Bandits" first appeared in an online issue of *Barrelhouse*, edited by Dan Brady and Tom McAllister.

"4.8.14" first appeared in *Elective Affinities*, edited by Carlos Soto-Román.

"7.22.14" was published in *Sugar Mule*, edited by Alyse Knorr.

"Snow Day" first appeared in *Bear Review*, edited by Marcus Myers and Brian Clifton. This poem quotes James Schuyler's "Empathy and the New Year."

"Saginaw (a documentary)" was first published under a different title in *The Fourth River*, edited by Sheila Squillante. The poem is in collaboration with Jaime Torres and features photographs from his series *New Plantation Blues*. This piece was written for a night titled "Someone was there to take a picture" at the Red Rover Reading Series in Chicago, IL, in 2009, and quotes the line "Someone was there to take a picture" from Kate Greenstreet's "56 Days."